T0124725

THE FATHER,
A son, A daughter,
A Love Affair

Charles R. Watson

ISBN: 978-1-4669-1646-3 (sc)
ISBN: 978-1-4669-1645-6 (e)

Trafford rev. 02/15/2012

 www.trafford.com

North America & international
toll-free: 1 888 232 4444 (USA & Canada)
phone: 250 383 6864 ♦ fax: 812 355 4082

TABLE OF CONTENTS

ACKNOWLEDGMENTS

No work is complete without the giving of thanks. Expressing gratitude to those whose assistance made this a better book. I am grateful for your generous support and sound advice: special thanks and appreciation to Gwendolyn Sims, and Susie Sansom- Piper:

Moreover I give thanks to God Almighty, for giving me the opportunity and privilege to write this book. My prayer, and expectation is that this book will be a insightful blessing, and an encouragement to all that read it.

INTRODUCTION

This love affair is based on the Word of God, the FATHER and His ultimate love in a relationship between the son and the daughter. It tells of a sincere love affair, a special communication telling how God brought the son and daughter together. Our love is complete through Christ. Truly God has performed an amazing, miraculous thing in our lives. Through our marriage covenant each partner is given equal rights that bring satisfaction to one another. Through this *testimony*, it is my sincere hope to spread joy to others.

I

God's Plan or Your Plan

Most men and women dream of having a beautiful relationship in their life. Only if it is put together by God, Himself can this type of relationship exist. What two people set out to make happen in a relationship on their own, is different from what God has endeavored for them. What God has provided is not the same. Why do people get in a big rush for nothing? Let God plan your life and not you, yourself.

It was in 1989- that I saw a young lady driving a bus, and I thought to myself, "she's beautiful" I would like to meet with her one day. It was love at first sight. But this was from the physical point of view. The real kind of love is that of the spirit of the heart, the God kind of love.

I did not realize that this was a part of God's plan, all the time.

I did not understand this in the spirit, at this time in my life. My thoughts of her were often although I did not know her. As time went by, I saw her every once in a while. Sometimes we are in a rush to have a mate; however we should wait on the Lord. If we learn not to complain God will see us through this time of waiting. We should seek out, and learn to be content, as we seek to hear God, for He's always speaking if we choose to be still and to listen to Him. God moved on my heart, and on the heart of the people of the agency in which she worked. Moreover God caused it to happen, after having two interviews; I soon received employment at the company, where she worked.

II

Identifying

God designed our life before we were ever born. He knew our long and short comings, of life. God knows everything we are going to do before we do it; the day, time, month, and the year. There's nothing God doesn't know about us, He is always at work to give us His best. Nonetheless, at times we lean to our own understanding, in our way of thinking. Yielding to God will put us on the right path. God hears what we do not hear. He understands what we do not understand. All we have to do is follow His lead. God speaks to us in dreams, visions, through people, and through His word, to guide His children and to protect them from danger. At times, we don't hear clearly, or wait on God. During this time in my life, some things could have been avoided.

But our waywardness doesn't stop the plan of God. However it can certainly delay it. *Matthew 19:6* said *Therefore what God has joined together let no man separate.* God does not have to defend His will or actions to anyone. God knows the heart and the intent of the heart. Once again "I say" God is always speaking, but on occasions we do not perceive, understand what He is saying. *Proverbs 3:5,6 Trust in the LORD with all your heart, and lean not on your own understanding; In all your ways acknowledge Him and He will direct your path.*

God is Spirit and life: yet He deals with us in mysterious ways. He allows suffering, through the chastening of those He love. *Revelation 3:19, Deut 8:5 Those whom I love I rebuke and discipline. So be earnest, and repent. Know then in your heart that as a man disciplines his son, so the Lord your God disciplines you.* We will suffer for the consequences of our disobedience; but repent, turning away from disobedience, is the way to be spared. Let us choose to walk in righteousness to receive benefits in the ways of the LORD. Holiness is the best and most beautiful thing there is. It cannot be seen with the natural eye, nor can it be touched with our physical being; but it is felt within the heart.

III

God Ordain Marriage

God's idea of marriage, is not man's idea of marriage, God's way is easier. What will we do without God's love? The LORD Himself shields, and protects us. He puts marriages together, and not you, yourself. *I Corinthians 7:36 said If anyone thinks he is acting improperly toward the virgin he is engaged to, and if she is getting along in years and he feels he ought to marry, he should do as he wants. He is not sinning. They should get married.*

One basic- and expected principle for a good marriage is each person must seek to please the other. God's idea of marriage biblically states, and constitutes in *Hebrew 13:4 Marriage should be honored by all, and the marriage bed kept pure, for God will judge the adulterer and all the sexually immoral.* Marriage is a covenant with God between the two people. It is also acknowledged and documented by public formal official and is recognized as a covenant. All believers should let God make the choice in whom to marriage. You should not attempt to make the choice on your own, this can be very damaging, both naturally and spiritually.

IV

Authorization
Release & Remarriage
(The authorization in marriage)

Marriage is permanent in the sight of God. Only from the hardness of man's heart was divorce put into place. *Deut 24: 1-4 If a man marries a woman who becomes displeasing to him because he finds something indecent about her, and he writes her a certificate of divorce, gives it to her and sends her from his house, and if after she leaves his house she becomes the wife of another man, and her second husband dislikes her and writes her a certificate of divorce, gives it to her and sends her from his house, or if he dies, then her first husband, who divorced her, is not allowed to marry her again after she has been defiled. That would be detestable in the eyes of the Lord. Do not bring sin upon the land the LORD your God is giving you as an inheritance.*

This was the Pharisees teachings under the law. And the Pharisees were attempting to entrap Jesus, with the violation of first century Judaism divorce. *Matt 19:3 Some Pharisees came to Him (Jesus) to test Him. They asked, is it lawful for a man to divorce his wife for any and every reason?*

Also in Mark 10:2 Some Pharisees came and tested Him by asking, is it lawful for a man to divorce his wife? The permit, to divorce is under the law and stressed by the law.

Thus Jesus clearly agreed with the Shummai School of interpretation. Divorce is put into place as a result of the hardness of man's heart. The phrase underscores the truth that divorce should only be a last resort. Sexual immorality, dishonesty, etc. causes hardness of the heart. Moreover, Jesus said in *Luke 16:18 anyone who divorces his wife and marries another woman commits adultery and the man who marries a divorced woman commits adultery. Matt 19:6B . . .So they are no longer two, but one therefore what God has joined together, let man not separate.* "I caution you, do not attempt to make this choice on your own, rather, allow God to choose for you.

Jesus said marriage was permitted from the beginning. *Matt 19:8 Jesus replied, Moses permitted you to divorce your wives because your hearts were hard. But it was not this way from the beginning.* Just as God brought Eve to Adam; *Genesis 2:22B,* "so He brought my wife to me".

The two schools of thought are:
1. Allowing divorce for virtually any reason
2. Denying divorce except on the grounds of adultery

The Pharisees undoubtedly expected Jesus to take one side, in which he would lose the support of the other side: friction. In our day and time, we behave alot like the Pharisees—the LAW, when we ought to be acting like Jesus - GRACE.

John the Baptist was imprisoned for his view on divorce and remarriage. *Matt 14:3 Now Herod had arrested John and bound him and put him in prison because of Herodias, his brother Philip's wife, for John had been saying to him: It is not lawful for you to have her* (your brother's wife)—LAW. Jesus set the proper ground rules for the discussion. The focus was not rabbinical interpretation, but the teaching of scriptures. *Matthew 5:31, 32 It has been said, anyone who divorces his wife must give her a certificate of divorce, but I tell you that anyone who divorces his wife except for marital unfaithfulness, causes her to become an adulterous, and anyone who marries the divorced woman commits adultery. I Corinthians 7:10 To the married I give this command (no not I but the Lord): A wife must not separate from her husband. But if she does, she must remain unmarried or else be reconciled to her husband. And a husband must not divorce his wife.* Divorce, has no part of God's original plan for marriage, which is one man be married to one woman for life.—GRACE.

The rabbinical stance regarding divorce; God's design for marriage is in the passage *Genesis 2:24 Christ quotes: For this reason a man will leave his father and mother and be united to his wife, and they will become one flesh.* And this passage of scripture presents four reasons for the inviolability, the blessedness of marriage.

1. God created, made, only two kinds of human being; *Gen 1:27B male and female He created them.* And God instituted marriage between a man and women at creation. Not groups of males, or groups of females; or those who share same sex partners as it please them. God forbid.
2. The word translated be joined, means to glue: this reflecting the strength of the marriage bond.
3. In God's eyes a married couple, is one flesh, male and female forming a single union; it's also the origin and manifestaton of reproduction.
4. God ordain marriage period, and it is not to be broken, ruined by man.

The release of marriage by death

Romans 7: 1-6 Know ye not, brethren, (for I speak to them that know the law,) how that the law hath dominion over a man as long as he lives? For the woman which hath a husband is bound by the law to her husband so long as he lives; but if the husband be dead she is loosed from the law of her husband. So if, while her husband lives, she be married to another man, she shall be called an adulterous: but if her husband be dead, she is free from that law; so that she is no adulteress, though she be married to another man. Wherefore, my brethren, ye also are become dead to the law by the body of Christ; that ye should be married to another even to him who is raised from the dead, that we should bring forth fruit unto God. For when we were in the flesh, the motions of sins, which were by the law, did work in our members to bring forth fruit unto death. But now we are delivered from the law, that being dead wherein we were held; that we should serve in newness of spirit, and not in the oldness of the letter.

Re-marriage

The hypothesis, theory is that divorcees will remarry. However if the divorce is not for sexual immortality: any remarriage is adultery. God does not acknowledge this order of divorce. That is why we should not trust in our own ability to seek a wife-/-husband for yourselves. God's way of marriage is permanent and enduring. Therefore, at all cost endeavor, to stay together, reconcile, to come to an agreement. Let divorce be last a resort. Christian Believers, particularly should follow God's order of remarriage. Reconcile with your mate, or remain unmarried.

We, as God's people, get into trouble, concerning marital matters; then expect God to bail us out: of these adulteress, remarried, sexual immortality, or divorce issues. Relationships and homes are being separated and destroy by the enemy, because we seek to find our own mate, instead of waiting on God for the right mate. Learn the teachings of Jesus, to avoid the mistake, of seeking your own mate.

V

My vision of the marriage

In my heart in reference to - *Habakkuk 2:2,3 Write down the vision and make it plain on tables so that read may run with it. For the vision is yet for an appointed time. And at the end it will not lie, so wait on the vision and it will come to pass*. It is God's appointed time, not your own. Trust and wait on God for your spouse.

God put our marriage together. However, when I first saw her, in 1989; it was not God's timing. Our Father was doing a beautiful job, painting a beautiful picture, bringing us together, in His timing. But, from (1989) to (1998) it appeared that God did nothing, to put this love affair together. Meanwhile, I acted out of my emotions, and wedded another.

Choices, choices, choices: the choice I made, led me into the wilderness. This caused me to suffer many things in my body. I had one horrific health condition after another. There are consequences for disobedience; perhaps this was mine. Although I could not have been with a nicer person, it was not God's will for me to marry this one. Sometimes we expect God to do what we want Him to do, when we want Him to do it. It does not work like that at all. I went off on the deep end, not waiting or trusting God. I know God will, and does answer prayer. Thus I kept seeking Him although I encountered many hardships. We do not understand, know, or realize what we are doing when we choose to do things our way. Every action has a reaction; the consequences of disobedience are never pleasant.

He who finds a wife finds a good thing, and obtains favor from the Lord. Proverbs 18:22; If it's not your good thing, it will usually end up in a divorce. And God hates divorce; it takes away from the foundation of family. God honors marriage. His design was never meant for man and woman to separate, or divorce for any reason except infidelity. Adverse difficulties may come, but we must keep the faith that line up with the word of God. *Philippians 4:13 - I can do all things through Christ, who strengthen me.* We as Christian believers should not marry an unbelieving person. *2 Corinthians 6:14 - Do not be unequally yoked together with an unbeliever. For what fellowship has righteousness with lawlessness? And what communion has light with darkness.*

If two unbelievers marry and one has commenced to believe, let the believer set an example. *I Corinthians 7:14a For the unbelieving husband is sanctified by the wife, and the unbelieving wife is sanctified by the husband.* And this is God's Divine Order.

In my heart of hearts, I've waited a long time for this moment, but in the depts of my mind, I had no idea that it would really happen. God knows our future and He knows our end. Finally, my first day after training, I saw her again at the bus stop: it was very satisfying though when I saw her. This was at my new job where we both were working. I had not spoke with her at all, and only saw her once in a while, for we had different work schedules. She did not know that I exist, but my eye was for her.

Now the time came when the LORD sent me to her with a word. When we first met I was shaking in my boots, so to speak; because of her great beauty. Even though I was hesitant, I had to do what God asked me to do. It was a while before we meet, I did not even know her name but, God was with me. When I told her what the LORD said in regards to her mother, she looked me directly in my eyes and these words came out of her mouth, it was only God that sent you with these words of wisdom. She thanked me, and gave me a hug at, this time my knees got a little weak, and my heart started racing. But when I look at her again I saw the Spirit of the LORD on her. I never looked at her again in any other way, only as a godly woman.

From this point on, when we saw each other, most of our conversation was primarily spiritual. Although we talked on several different occasions, I wanted to talk with her in a more personal way, but her facial appearance would throw me off, keeping me loss for words. This also kept me from having a personal relationship with her. I did not allow the LORD to continue to help me in this love affair and through my disobedience went in my own way. Over a period of time I got involved in a relationship with someone else, which cost me dearly. I did not take heed to the word of the Lord, when it was told to me not to marry this individual; I did it anyway so this marriage caused a stumbling block for both. Together we were in disobedience, and this is a serious offense toward God.

VI

Choose Obedience

One day I waited for her to come to work. While waiting, I was praying that God would help me with my communication skills. I did not want to be to direct, or forceful. When she arrived at work I walked her to the bus, and we began to talk. I told her if it is God's will, we will get together. I wanted to tell her how I felt about her. I had already prayed to God to help me with the words to say to her, but this was not the day or time.

One night a few weeks later she called and talked with my mother. After I came home, my mother and I talked about her. My mother told me that she had a nice conversation with her, also that she could hear wisdom and strength in her voice. I knew that my mother was very pleased with her. And I told my mother, that I had asked the LORD about getting together with her. And her reply was "wait on the LORD".

Approximately two months had passed, and I really needed to talk with her. On this occasion at the job, I met her in the hallway. I addressed her directly concerning my desires for this relationship. Moreover I told her how much I care, and loved her. Her response was that she was overwhelmed, regarding the feelings that I had for her. She also stated that she was seeing someone else. At this point I felt like a ton of brick had fallen on my heart. I was very hurt with this answer. After all, I knew that it was God who sent me to her. But her response caused me to turn away from what God said. I have already stated how disobedience is so costly. It is better to listen and obey God, and not lean to thoughts of foolishness.

II Timothy 3:6 speaks of gullible women . . . easy prey for the deceitful, false men or teachers. Persecution is coming to those who are disobedient to God's word and the law of grace and mercy. So, let every man and woman make every effort to live in self-discipline, and a obedient life unto God and His word.

I was hurt, and it caused me not to think soberly. My eyes were turned away from her, predicated upon her response, because she was seeing someone else. My actions caused me to walk in unrighteousness toward God, as I looked for comfort in another. I entered into a relationship with someone else, with the wrong attitude, knowing that there was no love there. And in a short time we decided to get married. I felt that I was really being unfair to her and to myself. I was not satisfied because it was not the person that I really love, and wanted to marry. On several different occasions I wanted to call it off. But, being the type of person that I am, I did not want to hurt her; so I entered a loveless marriage. However, I could not have been with a nicer person, but it was not God's choice or His perfect will for me.

Let me reiterate, on the argument of marriage and remarriage; only on the grounds of adultery is the divorce valid. If adultery is committed in the marriage, and one forgives the other then the marriage is still legitimate in the sight of God. Marriage is permanent with God; He has to orchestrate, decree, and bless the marriage. The law said we have to have license to be marry. Honoring the law of the land pleases God.

Now if a man loves his wife as Christ loves the church, God will bring great blessings from her. I thank God for giving me my wife; it took ten years for us to come together again, and it was well worth the wait. Praises unto God, He put a love affair back together, one that endured for Twenty years. Ten years before I ever spoke to her and ten years after I spoke with her. "I would like to say" I think that God kept her all this time just for me. On the other hand because of my decision I went into in my wilderness, and it was nothing pleasant, believe me.

VII

God's Timing

Thank God that He put the right woman in my life. From the very first time I saw her in nineteen eighty nine, I said to myself, Wow! I would like to marry her. So, over a period of time the LORD allow me to get a job, where we both worked together. I could see her face to face now, and she was very eye-catching to me. I would like to describe her; she has beautiful brown eyes, caramel type skin, and long golden dark brown hair. My desire was for us to be together. But it took nine more years before the LORD put this relationship and love affair together.

Point and time, clearly our timing is not God's timing. I had thoughts of what it would have been like if God had brought us together sooner. I soon dismissed this notion of thinking. If I had not detoured from the truth of what God was showing me concerning her, I would not have had a change of mind regarding marrying someone else.

Some men and women, who desire to enter into marriage, are fixed on what they set out to do. You cannot tell them anything. It's equally the same when two people are separating or getting a divorce. You can't say anything which would perhaps cause them to reconcile. Their minds are made up, and they are steady on course. I just wouldn't listen when my brother spoke to me. He said that the LORD spoke to him, telling him to tell me, not to marry the one I had chosen to marry. I just said to him, "ok, whatever." Even though I knew in my heart of hearts he was right. So, I struggled as I went down the path and chose not what God had in store for me.

After a period of time, I knew that God was all the while at work, both to will and do His good pleasure: causing my mind and my very being to line up with the will of His Word. The LORD revealed, related, and transformed, His truths to us as it regarded the above mentioned marriage. He also, so graciously allowed us to share what He had put in our hearts. After the time of sharing, we prayed together, we trusted the LORD to heal our hearts, to go forward, and be obedient to His will for our individual lives. By the Almighty hand of God, He delivered us, and by the Holy Spirit, caused us to go freely and willingly our individual ways.

Moreover God gave me His best, which was yet to come, in His time. A whole new life committed and devoted life to God, no longer going in my own way.

Sometimes, I think that I am dreaming: God waited on me, to be gracious to me. He put this love affair together: all I do is give thanks to Him, that we finally came together. She is truly a blessing from the LORD. I thank Him for her love inwardly and outwardly. She is my beautiful and spiritual wife. God is sovereign, and His word does not come back void, but accomplishes what it is sent out to do. I missed her, and my love was always for her, I continued to pray for her, and God answered my prayers. I thank God that I can live a whole new life with the woman that He gave me, a long time ago back in nineteen eighty nine, twenty years ago.

VIII

Continuing to Indentify

Men are providers naturally; a man provides for his wife because she is so intimately and inseparably connected to him. If he did not care for her, he would be diminishing his own glory which the wife brings to him by encouragement and submission. In marriage the two are so closely knit together, they are made one by the Holy Spirit of God. When the husband cares for the wife, he is also caring for himself. *Ephesians 5:2 said- walk in love.* In so doing this, we may please God.

We must sacrifice our bodies to the LORD, for He is in control of our life and our destiny: if we are willing to yield to Him and present ourselves as instruments of righteousness.

The word of God is true. It's a time to speak, although I spoke this "I believe I'll marry her" when I first saw her, I really didn't know at that time it was God, giving me the ability to speak these things. Now, "I can say" trust God for He is a rewarder of those that diligently seek Him. At the same time the LORD put me back on the right path; bless His Holy Name, I do not have to cry or be sad any more. It was all working together for my good. And now I am about to get married, to the one He gave me. To a wonderful woman and a God sent wife, I thank God for, everything He has done, and is doing in my life. I thank God for keeping her, (my wife) for hiding her in the cliff of the rock, for such a time as this. I am learning to be obedient to Him.

This is what perfect love is all about; being in obedience. To me and to her, love is from God Himself: He orchestrated the love of this relationship and continues to give it life. Anything less than God's perfect love is what you are doing on your own. If you go in your own way, you might just get a surprise, and that surprise will not be nice, I know this from personal experience. Trust in God, believe Him, wait on Him, and He'll bring you through the storms of life.

As born again believers, men and women must wait on God for their companion. Let the Lord God choose the right mate for you. He knows who He has for you, and it is His best for you. Don't let your heart be hardened to go in your own way; to look at what you want physically. As some would say, marriage is viewed to a good looking man or a beautiful woman, wanting someone with a nice shape or figure, a person with lots of money or possessions, etc., etc. Acquisitive things should not be what causes' you to want to be with a person. The heart of the matter should be to love, moreover a continual learning to love more.

It does not pay to be ignorant all of your life; but it does pay to be rightfully aware, indentify. Our Father strictly shows us how to live a healthy well-balanced life, so be patient, and wait on the LORD. Evil is never caused by God. *Ezekiel 14:5b . . . because they are all estranged from Me by their idols.* He does permit suffering to punish the unrepentant- to encourage sinners to repent, and to purify the righteous. Materialistic, intellectual, idolatry: the lust of the flesh, the lust of the eye, and the pride of life, are of those choosing to walk in ignorance, disbelieve, and or disobedience. God will allow your sin to run its course: because of the spirit of idolatry that is in the heart.

After sin run its course, which is only distinguished by God Almighty, your heart will be seized, by Him for a restorative purpose. God loves us. *Proverbs 3:12a For whom the Lord loves He corrects, just as a father the son in whom he delights. Rev 3:19 As many as I love, I rebuke and chasten. Therefore be zealous and repent.* He will see you through, strengthen you and give you the desire, aspiration He has put in your heart. Only be patient, and wait on the LORD.

I wish that I had more patience to lean and trust the things that God had given to me during that time in my life. I suffered many things, but God, in His mercy, grace, love, and power, allowed me to experience comfort, by the Holy Spirit in the mist of it. I finally let go, of doing it my way, and let God have His way. Now, I've learned, and I am learning still to walk in the ways of the LORD, it is safer. Consequently without the LORD'S help I was doomed for failure. I'm learning to trust and obey the LORD for He directs my path.

In the word of God: *Hebrew 13:4,5 Marriage is honorable and the bed undefiled; but God will judge the sexually immoral and adulterous. Keep your life free from love of money and be content with what you have, for He said I will never leave you or forsake you.* He draws us, with love, and convicts our hearts to righteousness. Conviction said- not this, but that. And this show forth the love of God and how He waits (on us) to be gracious to us. God instituted marriage between a man and women at creation thus signifying that marriage is honorable.

God design sexuality and it is intended to bond the man and woman together in marriage. When sexual acts are performed outside of marriage it destroys the outlook of unity in intimacy: which is to bond the man and woman experientially in every facet of the married. When sex is only an act physically, the relationship between the two has lost it's power to properly bond and be relational with each other. It is not just the physical portion of the marriage that is to be gratified and fulfilled. God's design is wholeness to the spirit- the heart of man, the soul- the psychological, the body- physical of all mankind. Complete unity and harmony of His created beings.

The LORD God called to Adams, where are you! Genesis 3:9 . . . Adams had broken his companionship, fellowship with God. Is God calling you, asking, where are you . . . have you broken your relationship with God through disobedient as it relates to His word? Wrong choices—sin separate us from God. The Almighty God, the creator of the universe and of the entire human race, loves His created beings so MUCH! Even in our state of blunder, or disobedience He waits on us to be gracious to us, to restore us to complete fellowship and relationship, unto Himself.

Do not bring a single mentality into a married relationship. It will bring bitterness into the relationship. God desire for man/woman to be whole and complete, and that the heart would be healed of all wounds. We are so very special to God, and He loves us so much. There is great hope in His name. Jesus the healer, protector, provider, and deliverer, knows what we stand in need of.

I made it through by the LORD Jesus Christ. It was hard being without the woman, I truly loved. I always prayed for her that God would put her in the path of righteous woman that would help her on her way. So that her Christian walk would match her talk, as well as her helping others to see the light of God in her. I thought I would never see her again. I did not know where she was in this world, but God knew where she was. I slightly felt like God was preparing us for when we would come together. So when He bought us together, it took us out of our minds, because it was and is spiritual. It's a beautiful and most gracious relationship, which I've ever known in this life: this was God's plan from the being, concerning this love affair. It was lost unto me for a while but God put it back together again; truly God has blessed this relationship, and orchestrated this marriage. We have truly found favor with God, both of us thank Him for blessing us with His righteousness and faithful obedience unto Him. God has changed my life in so many ways. I thank Him for opening my eyes and giving me understanding in this area of my life.

IX

We Are Not Our Own

God knows what best for those that are in leadership position, as it regards to the House of God. All men must wait on the LORD for their wife, but especially those in leadership- Pastors, deacons, and evangelists. These wives should be of God's choosing and not of one's self, it could be dangerous. A Christian wife need to submit to her husband whether he is a Christian or not. In this salvation can come, through submission. *I Peter 3:1 said wives be submissive to your own husband . . . I Peter 3:7* states- *God told man to give honor to the wife as to the weaker vessel . . .* the definition for weaker- is that women are physically weaker and in need of protection, provision, and strength from her husband. The husband needs to offer his loving duties, and to be sensitive to her needs. In addition she is fully equal in Christ and not inferior spiritually.

Ecclesiastes 9:9 states: "Live joyfully with the wife whom you love all the days of your life". A godly woman, that is in Christ Jesus and that loves Him, will submit herself to God; and also submit to her husband. Submission to God first, causes a like submit to her husband. Men build up your wife in the LORD, learn to pray for her, give time- (in the reading and studying of the Word of God together) and love her always; by this your household will be blessed by the LORD.

I suffered because I did not want to wait, but I learned, and I am still learning to wait on Him for everything. My whole life is better now by the Holy Spirit of God. *I John 2:16 states-For all that is in the world, the lust of the flesh, and the lust of the eye, and the pride of life is not of the Father, but is of the world.* Don't let lust rule; it will take you further than you want to go, keeps you longer than you want to stay, and cost you more than you want to pay, truly I know.

The love that I have for her is incredible. It was, and is God given. Being without her, at times was hard to bear, but I endure the pain of missing her day and night, and year after year. This kind of love goes past earthly, fleshly love. It is heavenly love that comes from God. Thank God in spite of myself, my life is better now. We all must suffer the consequence for the choices we make. God will strengthen us beyond intellectual and physical dimensions, for all believers that are serious about Him and His word.

Thank God for His anointing that He has put on both of our lives'; the love, peace, joy and understanding that we have with each other, that only God can give. He has given us power to submit to Him, and to one other. This is what makes our relationship so special; between, the Father, the son, the daughter and this love affair. Now I do not have to cry, nor am I lonely anymore, because God fixed this relationship His way, and that's what makes it so exceptional. Truly, I thank God that He put the relationship on hold for this point and time. It is so much better now. At that time neither one of us was mentally, emotionally capable to be together. When God join two people together He is the glue that bonds the two together. He made us ready for this love affair. The Lord has strengthened, and is strengthening us in so many ways . . . spirit, soul and body. Moreover when God orchestrates marriage, there will not be a divorce or remarriage in the relationship.

X

Our Life Is In Christ

We now have a beautiful relationship, and a excellent life in the LORD. We are always pressing to be obedient, to keep the faith, and the Word of the LORD: God helps us to overcome the challenges that are in our life. I let the rings of my life go, and I let God take control. I have kept and do keep believing and trusting God: He has bought, and is continuing to bring about change, inside out. I was standing on *Hebrews 11:6 But without faith it is impossible to please Him; and Romans 14: 23 whatever is not of faith is sin.* I trust God Almighty, the pieces of the puzzle are together, and my life is complete in this love affair.

Sometimes we never know what God will do, or not do. We should recognize that He is a righteous and Holy God, therefore we must continue to trust Him. Thank God for correcting, and refining me in His sovereignty. He has given me the grace to line up with His will, to receive my wife. She has truly been a blessing to me, and God knew this all along. A lot of times I would wonder where she was and is she still walking it the faith. Now, I can say that the LORD has truly watched over and kept her. I thank God for keeping both of us in good health and young at heart. Please understand that it is not healthy or fruitful to be in a relationship that

God has not put together. It is hazardous to your health, Christian or non-Christian.

As a born again believer's men and women know that we are not to kiss, or be sexually active, pending marriage: it loses its power to bond the two together. But we have gotten so caught up in the ways of the world, that we have ignored what the Word of God saids. By this, we have given over to the world's way of thinking, and acting, and not the LORD's way. By His Almighty hand my life is acceptable, before Him. God has put me and "the love of my life" together which He has given me.

Before we were officially united, we would talk hours and hours on the phone very intimately. We talk about some old things and definitely, some potential new experience. All at the same time the LORD was blending us together with cores of love in the spirit. This relationship was not lost or forgotten, and if my mother were here to see this day, she would rejoice.

Now we are engaged Praise God, it's with the love of my life. She is so gracious and beautiful in my eyes. I am well pleased with the choice that was made for me. I am the happiest man in the world at this point and time in my life. I am truly blessed. It is hard to express the wonderful shared love with the one I really love. She is full of wisdom and knowledge. I can see a glimpse of the image of God's love, in her life. She walks with the LORD, she talks like Him and you can tell that God has given her His wisdom. This is a special jewel from God, which He has given to me; like a diamond and a pearl all together in one.

She is now my mate, my lover, my support and companion. I love being with her, and around her. She is full of laughter, and joy, and it has brought happiness to both our lives. By God from the beginning to end, this love is for eternity.

Surely this is the God kind of love from heaven. Truly this is God's doings in bring us together.

Believers should have an ongoing passion, to stay in fellowship with the LORD God Almighty. He will show you yourself and reveal His truths. Changed agents transformed inwardly; putting into practice an outward manifestation of the fruit of the Spirit. Let us always have a posture of genuine reverence toward God. A life of adoration brings about healing to the heart, healing from the pass that you may walk in the future, of your destiny.

Apple of my eye, she is, and my soul mate for life. I live and breathe for the LORD and her too. She is the very thing that a man desire to find in a woman. God, put us side by side according to His plan, and for His purpose. Now, we share this joy and union of living together in our hearts with one another. It is a new beginning and a joy; it is also a celebration of life, sharing our destiny together. There are family and friends that celebrate with us too.

We are trusting God, that our relationship will always grow stronger day by day, by the grace of God and Spirit of God. As we continue to walk with the LORD He will strengthen us on our journey. It was only a matter of time before the LORD would unite and consecrate our hearts and spirits together. And now we have agreed to love one another always. The greatest gift is love, God is Love. Our greatest submission to each other is love, through Christ Jesus our LORD.

I Corinthians 7:4-7 For the wife does not have authority over her own body, but the husband does. Likewise the husband does not have authority over his own body, but the wife does. Do not deprive one another, except perhaps by agreement for a limited time, that you may devote yourselves to prayer; but then come together again, so that Satan may not tempt you because of your lack of self-control. Now as a concession, not a command, I say this, I wish that all were as I myself am. But each has his own gift from God, one of one kind and one of another.

God has blessed us with His Son, His word, His love, and the Holy Spirit; whom has comforted our hearts. Our marriage is on the right road, and we are moving toward our destiny, in Christ Jesus. Both of us are as children (open) before God, living together and life is good. Keep in mind, nothing on this side of heaven is perfect. God's love is perfect, and His love continues to cases away all fear in our lives. Let the rings of your life go and the LORD will take control of it.

Before we were united, I gave the LORD the rings of my life; and I am continuing to be changed to His image. The LORD reached way down inside of me, and pulled everything out that was not like Him. He changed me from the inside out. I just love how the LORD does things. Truly, I know that there is nothing to hard for the God. The LORD show me how one can be deceived, by believing the lie. The previous marriage was a lie from the very beginning. After being together a while, one night the LORD asks me, how long was I going to be disobedient, and to tell her the truth: He also reintegrated that a liar would not tarry in His sight.

Wow! Are my thoughts at times, this is unbelievable it seems unreal, too good to be true, impossible, and unimaginable, to the natural mind. Occasionally I just sit, look, and think, after twenty years the LORD brought us together, and all I can say is, how Great is are God. It is God that arms me with strength, and makes my way right in His sight. I'm learning to trust Him in the difficult circumstances from day to day. I don't trust my feeling, I trust my LORD to carry us through each day.

We've have been married for a several months. I've come to realize and appreciate, that she is the same loving person at heart, and this is a great comfort to me. I am grateful and thankful that we can share the word of God in dept with each other. God could not have given me a better mate, to help me in ministry and in my life. I adore her, cherish her, and her presence overwhelms me. I love being around her, and the intimacy that we have with each other. She is the one I talk to in peace, walk with in love, understanding more with joy, she is a blessing. However we are not perfect people. We just have the fear God, and do reverence of Him. Our desire is to worship Him more and always. Thank God for His favor with us. He has given and is giving us grace in submission to follow and obey Him. This pleases the LORD, and it pleases us too.

Let me, urge or advises you, to remember that life is short, it is precious, and every moment counts. It is crucial that one does not go outside the will of God seeking a mate, but be patient and wait on Him. Be careful, to not let your flesh or intellect get in the way of the will of God, remember our thoughts are not His thoughts, nor our ways His ways. Let us keep humble before the LORD as dear children, that we might keep a relationship with Him clear to hear Him. The world is an enemy to God, and to those that are His. Ask, God to let you be the answered pray to a husband, or a wife.

Pray, pray, pray, press on to pray diligently, with all types of prayers and supplication; pray without creasing, pray always. Prayer is talking to God; it is our fellowship with Him, and our relationship. It is our privilege to pray; to watch and pray. Time with the Father is of the essence. Do not let the enemy, (Satan) stop you, or steal your time of prayer. Always make time to be with the LORD JESUS CHRIST, who die that we might have this right, to this sweet communion with Him. It does not matter how short the prayer. If we are His . . . like a parent waits to hear the child's words so the Father hearkens to hear our words. And He speaks back to us.

Charles R. Watson

My prayer for you is to stay strong in the power of His might, be wise as a serpent, but harmless as the dove. May God bless you, and may His Spirit lead you in all He has given you to do, as it regards a sufficient other.

Printed in the United States
By Bookmasters